George Colman

The Suicide

A Comedy

George Colman

The Suicide
A Comedy

ISBN/EAN: 9783741199790

Manufactured in Europe, USA, Canada, Australia, Japa

Cover: Foto ©Andreas Hilbeck / pixelio.de

Manufactured and distributed by brebook publishing software (www.brebook.com)

George Colman

The Suicide

The Suicide

a Comedy.

Theatre Royal.

Hay Market.

Prologue.

'Tis now the reigning taste, with Belle and Beau.
Their Art and Skill in Coachmanship to shew
Nobles contend, who throws a Whip the best
From Head to Foot, like Hackney Coachmen Drest
Duchess and Peeress too discard their fear
Ponies in front, my Lady in the rear
A Female Pheaton all danger mocks
Half Coat— half petticoat, She mounts the box
Wrapt in a dusty Whirlwind scours the plains
And Cutting — Jehu! — whistling, holds the reins
Happy, thrice happy Britain is thy State
When each Sex drives, at such a furious rate
The modish Artist, play wright or Coach maker
In Grub street Starv'd, or thriving in Long Acre
To suit the Times and tally with the mode
Must travel in the beaten Turnpike road
Wherefore our Crane neck'd Manager to day
Upon four Acts, attempts to run his Play
A fifth he fears wou'd deem the Bards reproach
A meer fifth Wheel, that wou'd but Stop the Coach

With two Act pieces what Machines agree
Buggies — Tim-whiskies, or Squeez'd Vis a Vis
Where two Sit Face to Face, and knee to knee.
What is a piece in one short act comprest
A Wheel barrow — or Sulky at the best
A Scale so small the bard wou'd suffer fo't
You'd say his Farce was like himself — too short.
Yet anxious with your Smiles, his work to Crown
In many a Varied Shape he courts the Town
Sometimes he drives — if brother bards implore
Sometimes he in a Prologue, trots before
Or in an Epilogue gets up behind
Happy in all, so you appear but kind
His Vehicle to day may none reproach
Nor take it for a Hearse or Mourning Coach
'Tis true, a gloomy outside he has wrought
Than rather threatens than doth promise ought
Yet from black funeral like his brother bays
A nuptial Banquet he intends to raise
We do but jest — poison in jest — no more
And thus one Mercer to the World restore
But if a well tim'd Jest shou'd chance to save
One Mercer from Perdition and the Grave

Ludgate Hill be judge if twere not hard
to dese shou'd you bring in the Bard.

Dramatis Personæ.

Tobine	Mr Palmer
Tabby	Aickin
Dr Truby	Blissett
Catchpenny	Baddeley
Ranter	Bannister
Bounce	Webb
Squib	R. Palmer
Wingrave	
Juggins	Massey
Bolus	

Waiters, Watchmen Servants &c.

~~John~~
~~Anthony~~
~~Tom~~

Mrs Grogram	Mrs Webb
Nancy	Mrs Lloyd
Maid	Miss Hale

The Suicide
Act 1st

(1) Watchman, John, Peggy}

(2) Mrs Grosicam}

(3) John, Nancy}

{ Table. 2 Chairs / 2 Candles — on

Scene New Chamber.

A Man & Maid sitting on each side of a Table fast asleep.

Watchman (without)

Past five o'clock! — five o'clock, — and a cloudy Morning. — Past five —— o'clock. {a violent Rapping at PSdoor. A Cloudy Morning. ————— Rap again.

Maid (waking)

Ma'am! Sir,! Yes! coming (Rap again) bless me, here's Somebody at the Door, I'll go and let them in. *Takes the Candle & Going- Stops*

But why shou'd I go, and that Fellow sitting asleep! It may be Thieves for ought I know, and a Man is the fittest to deal with them — Here you John. — fast as a Church — D'ye hear John? The Fellows dead I think ————— (Shakes him)

John (waking)

What! what! —ha Peggy! Give me a Kiss Love!
Maid.
Pshaw! foolatum! have done with your nonsense and go to the Door
John.
Go, to the Door!—Go to Bed, I say. (pulling her)
Maid.
I won't be haul'd (Rap again) there! there! d'ye hear?
John.
I neither hear, nor see any thing but you my Love (rap)
Maid. breaking from him)
Why does not the Fellow go? They'll beat the Door down.—It's my Young Master I suppose.
John.
Well, let him beat the door down, or turn the House out of the Windows — just as he pleases. Any Change must be for the better, I am sure my old Master Tabby is so fond of early Hours, and Young Squire Tobine is so given to late Ones there's no regularity in this Family. A poor Servant has no Comfort between them, and if it was not for my pretty Peggy here

Maid.
Be quiet then! — We shall have the whole House in an Uproar (Rap again) See there — here's Madam Grogram, as sure as I'm alive.

Enter Mrs Grogram. OP

Mrs Grog.
Why John! why Peggy! — arn't you asham'd hussey to have that idle Fellow pulling and stopping you about in that Fashion.

Maid.
I'm sure, Ma'am I was only pressing him to go to the Door.

John.
Indeed Ma'am, I was only just ——

Mrs Grog.
Go to the door — Will you let your Master wait all day for you?

John.
We have been waiting all night for him Madam.

Mrs Grog.
No more Words, but go to the Door Man. (*John goes & [soon] returns with Nancy in hand &c &c*)

John.
M.r Rattle, Ma'am.

M.rs Grog.
Oh is it you M.r Rattle? I have something to say to you — Go both of you and wait in the next Room a little — d'ye hear. —

John.
Yes, Ma'am — Umph! — Umph — Come along Peggy. umph! — umph! ——————— Exit with Peggy OP

Manet M.rs Grogram & Nancy.

M.rs Grog.
Well, Sir,' — Or well, Madam! for I hardly know what to call you, or, what to say to you — Is your Wild goose Chace almost over yet?

Nancy.
We are in full View, and full cry at this Moment Madam.

M.rs Grog.
You are a keen Sportsman, truly Miss.

Nancy.
And why not my dear Madam? How many of my Young Female Acquaintance in the Country, fly

over Hedges, and Ditches. Leap five-bar Gates, Scramble up Hill, and down; from Fallow to Greensward in pursuit of a Hare, or, a Fox, a Man is my Object. the Game is nearly run down, and like other Ladies in the Field, I hope to save it from the Dogs instead of being in at the Death.

Mrs Grog.

As to saving him his Fortune at least — there are scarce any hopes of it. And as to yourself, tho' our good friend Dr Truby who attended you to the very brink of the Grave, as we thought assur'd me there was no other way of saving your Life

Nancy.

Nay, don't fly off, now we're in the very heart of the business Madam.

Mrs Grog.

Your heart has been almost broken in the Course of it, Nancy. — And yet if the Doctor had not made himself a party in this mad project, a poor Weak Woman

woman, or foolish fond Godmother as I am.
and he always calls me   I should never
have winked at it, much less have consented
to join it; I assure you Nancy.

Nancy.
The kindness of your Motive my dear Madam
was evident, and be assur'd it will answer
You have restor'd my Health and Spirits already.
you see, and whenever I resume the Petticoat;
and become Nancy Lovell again, I do not
doubt of your rejoicing at the happy turn of
my Adventures in the Character of Dick Rattle.

Mrs Grog.
I see very little prospect of it at present, Dick,
Nancy.

Nancy.
The Prospect will clear: Do but indulge me in
this frolic. — It is the last request, I shall urge
Madam.

Mrs Grog.
Nay, I never had any Objection to a Frolick
If any good was like to have come of it, nor

ever had any aversion to pleasure, taken as it ought to be, I was always as ready for a ball at Lord Mayors,—a Feast at Guildhall, a party to Hampstead, or Trip to Margate, as any Woman in the City: but Young Mr Tobines Conduct is out of all reason—And if it was not for my dear dead Mr Grograms other partner, Mr Tabby, whom the whole Town knows to be good as the Bank, and firm as the Monument, the poor Hen and Chickens that have been the pride of Bucklersbury for more than these fifty Years wou'd be Whereas'd in the Gazette in less than a fortnight.

<u>Nancy.</u>
You are mistaken, believe me Madam. I shou'd be miserable indeed from my dotage on Mr Tobine, if I was not convinc'd that he had the best Heart in the World — that very goodness of Heart join'd to a ____. fatal turn for genteel pleasures, have laid him open to dangers which make me tremble- and which I have never dar'd to disclose to you.

Mrs Grog.

Dangers! what Dangers? Sure he has not thought of absconding, or altering Figures in his accounts? Or —

Nancy.

Dangers that affect no-body, but himself I assure you — He is too honest to hurt any body else — but press me no further to mention any thing to his prejudice — My present disguise is too convincing a proof of my partiality for him —— We have been acquainted from Children you know; and our mutual regard has grown up insensibly with us.

Mrs Grog.

Insensibly with a Witness — At least on your part. The Man's undone, Nancy.

Nancy.

I hope not. — I am as Sensible as yourself of his Follies and Weaknesses, and have form'd this plan to wean him from them.

Mrs Grog.

By joining him in his Extravagance. A Strange

way of weaning by encouraging his Intemperan.
Nancy.

Nancy.
Mix but a little Wormwood with the gratificatio.
of it, and its the only effectual way. Madam.

Mrs Grog.
And when do you apply this Wormwood you
speak of?

Nancy.
All in good Time, Madam. In the mean while
a Surfeit may forward our purpose.

Mrs Grog.
But in the mean while he'll die of the Surfeit.

Nancy.
Nay leave my patient to me, I beseech you
Madam. consider too, that I have our friend
Dr Truby, a most Skilful Physician to consult
on my operations. The disorder is now brought
to a Crisis: The Doctor and I are of the College.
and we'll work a cure, I warrant you.

Mrs Grog.
Like all the rest of the College, Kill, or Cure, I

I suppose

{ 4
John
Peggy }

Nancy.
No Cure, no Pay. I have felt his pulse, and it beats very high, I assure you. Not half an hour ago, I left him in a high fever, with every Cause and Symptom of Inflamation about him — the best Thing you can do is to put him to Bed, as soon as possible.

Mrs Grog.
What! coming home in the Old Way I suppose."

Nancy.
In his old Way, and with his Old Friends, Ranter, and Catchpenny, the Author & Actor. but had not we better retire, before he arrives Madam? He'll be for beginning the Evening again, and calling for Wine, if he finds me up, perhaps; for tho' but a new acquaintance, I am a violent favorite; and it is by his invitation, not yours, that I sleep here remember.

Mrs Grog.
Amidst all his pranks, I must say that for him..
you

You are the only Miss, he ever brought home with him.

Nancy.

And Me, not as a Miss, you know, It will be some little Surprize I believe, when he finds how often I have slept in his House, by his own Appointment.

Mrs Grog.

Go, you're a mad Girl, but a good Heart, I'll answer for you.

5)
1 Tobine
2 Ranter
3 Catchpenny
& others with
Ensigns
Chorus
Watchmen
Band &c

Nancy.

And he's a mad Spark! but honest, take my word for it.   _ Exeunt. PS _

Re=Enter Man & Maid OP.

John.

So, so; so; to be sure I see nothing, I hear nothing and I know nothing. ———{Ready to break Windows

Maid.

Why what have you seen or heard, or what do you know Mr. Wise acre?

John.

Oh nothing, nothing at all not I, Servants

Servants must be Deaf, Dumb, and Blind you know Peggy.

Maid.

Why for that matter, least said (as they say) is soonest mended.

John.

I say nothing. I am glad to find Madam Grogram, has all her Eye Teeth tho' – Aye and a Colts tooth or two into the Bargain – The Gentlewoman can mumble a bit of upper crust, still I believe – I wish she don't get into bad Bread here tho' – for this Young Rattle is but a kind of Farthing Role – not your genuine Household – the true Standard according to act of Parliament – Between You, and Me Peggy.

{ *Noise without of breaking Windows* }

Maid

Mercy on us, the Old trade again.

John.

Yes yes Master Tobine is coming home now, you may be sure. Come, we'll go and let him in Peggy. and take care to shut out his Companions.

Exeunt PS.

{Wing Bell} — {Lamps down
(Whistle) Scene Changes to the Outside
of the House. Tobine, Grogram, Tabby
in Large Golden Letters on Front. PS.
Enter Ranter, Catchpenny, and Others bearing
the Ensigns of Comus's Court. (All drunk.)

Catch:
Toby, come along Toby! Here is thy Mansion my boy
The glory of Silkworms, and the Gentleman's and
Lady's Magazine! Here is thy Castle.

Ranter.
Ay, come along my old Lad of the Castle; We have
brought the Trophies of Comus's Court from the
Club Room, and you shall make your Triumphal
Entry, like Alexander into Babylon.

Enter Tobine &c hauling the City Waits in PS

Tobine.
Here are Pipers, and Scrapers, and Scrapers, for you
my boys! Wind and Catgut for ever, a jolly
night and a merry Christmas for ever, I say

~~Musician~~
~~But Gentlemen.~~

Ranter. [flings one,... others ...]

Play away then Fiddles, and Hautboys; play away Rascals.

Catch:

That they shall. Come, blow pipers, like a Chubby Cheek'd Boreas at the Corner of an Old Picture! And Fiddlers Scrape till your Elbows Ach again.

Tobine.

Oh, rare Catchpenny! Now Master Ranter, whats your Midsummer Nights Dream, to a good Winters Evening? — London and December for my Money; the shortest Day, and the longest Night forever, I say.

Catch.

Well, said, little Toby! why you're the very genius of a happy New Year — all Holly, and Ivy — Ivy — an Exact Emblem of Christmas.

Ranter.

An Abstract and brief Chronicle of the Times, my boy.

Tobine

Hark ye Catchpenny! You're a Poet, here are the Waits ready, and if you are lirically inclin'd, You may give us an Ode to some tune you see.

"'Twas at the Royal Feast in Persia won"..

Catchp.

I'll tell you what Toby. I'll make a better Ode than Alexanders Feast. Extempore. — Dryden was no-body — not a Spark of true Poetical Fire in his whole Composition — and as to Pindar — I'd Spin better Odes than Pindar by a Versification of Weatherby's Racing Calender.

Ranter.

Little Catchpenny.

Cath.

What dost thou say my Boy.?

Ranter.

Don't you be jealous now, Old Dryden and Pindar there's the Bell-man speaking his Verses yonder — but don't let it make you uneasy I say.

Catch:

Why, thou blood of a Scene Shifter! thou vile Murderer of Blank Verse! engender'd between a Dancing Devil, and a Tragedy Princess. dost thou think that my Poetry. was ever announc'd by a Bell.

like your former Exhibitions in the Country with a Trumpet.

Tobine.

Plague on you both, and your Acting and Poetry together! there's the Music sheering off Yonder. What Signifies bringing the Trophies, if we don't make the Sheets Ring again?

Ranter.

I'll warrant you Squire — Come back you Scound. Come Rascals, play us a Tune, fit for those noble accompanyments! — I say a moving Club! Eh Squire? *Pointing to the Trophies*

Tobine.

Ay, give us one noble Crash, One full Chorus, And then perhaps we may let you go without breaking your Heads Scoundrels.

Catch.

Let's have my last new Song Toby.

Toby.

So we will — Sing it Ranter. — Strike up Musick.

Song

If Life is a Bubble and breaks with a blast
You must toss off your Wine, if you'd wish it to last
For the Bubble may well be destroy'd with a Puff
If 'tis not kept floating in Liquor enough

2

If Life is a Flow'r as Philosophers say
'Tis a very good hint understood the right way
For if Life is a Flow'r any Blockhead can tell
If you'd have it look fresh, you must moisten it well

3

This Life is no more than a Journey 'tis said
Where the Roads for most part are confoundedly bad
Then let Wine be our Spur and all Travellers will own
That whatever the Roads, we jog merrily on.

4

This World to a Theatre liken'd has been
Where each Man around has a part in the Scene
'Tis our part to be Drunk, and 'tis matter of Fact
That the more you all drink Boys the better you'll act

5

This Life is a Dream in which many will weep
Who have strange silly fancies, and will cry ▓▓▓
But of us when we wake from our Dream, 'twill be said
That the Tears of the Tankard, were all that we shed.

End of Song Enter W...

Tobine.
A Ghost! a Ghost!
Ranter.
Angels and Ministers of Grace defend us.
Watchman.
Ain't you asham'd, to disturb the Sober honest Neighbourhood in this disorderly manner? You ought to be made to give an account of your selves
Ranter.
What may this mean? that thou pale Ghost Revisit'st thus the Glimpsies of the Moon, Making Night hideous
Watchman.
Hideous! why hideous.
Catch.
I'll tell you what, Toby. with his Long Pole, and his Lanthorn; he puts me in mind of Old Time with his Scythe, and his Hour Glass.
Watchman.
Hour Glass!— I cry the Hour to be sure
Tobine.

Tobine
Why harkee Old Fellow? — Dost thou think that with that Lath of a Carcase, and that Dagger of Lath in thy Hand, thou wilt be able to Cope with this Company.

Watch.
It was some of this Company, I fancy, that lock'd me up tother-night fast asleep in my Watch box.

Ranter.
You're Right Old Starlight and Moonshine! we lock'd you up tother night in your Sleep, sure enough, and to-night we'll lock you up again broad awake, my boy.

Catch.
Come little Toby, lay hold of him.

Watch:
Oh! if that's the Case, I'le soon be a Match for you
Snakes his Lanthorn — Rattle heard
Enter a Possee of Watchmen

Catch:
An irruption of the Goths, and Vandals — Fall on my boys.

Ranter &c. Overpower'd by the Watchmen.

Ranter.

'Confusion: baffled, by a base born hind!'

2.^d Watch.

Not so base born as yourself, may hap – Come along my Masters! You shall go to the Round House, for the present, and then before the Alderman, at Guildhall, or the Mansion House

1.st Watch.

We'll teach you to put Padlocks upon Watchboxes

2.^d Watch.

We'll make you pay Sauce I warrant you.

Ranter.

Oh! I am fortunes Fool.

Exeunt: PS

Drop 1.st Chamber] [End of Act 1.st]

Then when Ready drop Curtain

{ Saloon }
{ Wings }

Act 2d { Curtain drop to discover }

1st Chamber — a Chamber
{ (1) Tobine John }

Tobine at Breakfast.

Tobine

Come, another Bowl of Tea

As to their Bread and Butter, and dry Toast, I could as soon Eat, or digest a deal Board. Getting Tipsey over-night is pleasant enough; but its a devilish disagreeable Operation; the Sobering Oneself again the next Morning — And this meagre Slop does me no good neither.

Enter John PS

Make me a Doctor and put a Spoonfull Extraordinary of Brandy, and a good deal of Nutmeg in it, d'ye hear. I'm cursed Sick I doubt our Wine, last { Exit John } night was not genuine, and then that damn'd Bowl of Arrack Punch and Jellies with the broil'd Beef-bone, at three in the Morning quite overset me — But the Women

Women would call for it — Let me see — What says the News. ⟨...⟩ Egad who knows but I may supply matter for a Spirited Paragraph one of these Mornings (looking at it) What's here, Modern Characters by Shakespear. (Reads)

{ "The People of E— dash — d—ay— England no doubt He shall recover his Wits there, or, if he don't it's no great matter — for there the folks are all as mad as he. (Wrote)

"Hamlet. Act 5ᵗʰ" { (2) Tabby

His M— dash —y
Ay every Inch a ———
      ·   <u>Enter John.</u>
          <u>John</u>
The Doctor, Sir.
          <u>Tobine.</u>
Very well, Set it down.
          <u>John.</u>
A Lady in the Shop desires to see you, Sir.
          <u>Tobine</u>
Bid Prig the Foreman speak to her
          <u>John.</u>
He has, Sir, but she must speak to you she says.

Tobine.
Tell her I'm not at home.
John.
They have told her you are at home already, Sir.
Tobine.
Say, I am not well.
John.
She'll let no body serve her but yourself, Sir.
Tobine.
Is she pretty John?
John.
An Old Lady, Sir!
Tobine.
Than old Tabby may do for her, desire him to wait on her.
John.
I shall Sir. .. Exit PS
Tobine.
And now let me return to my Studies.—Let me see! Ah plague, I'm so dizzy the Letters all Swim before me [...] I begin to be tir'd of my own Company

I'll send to see if Dick Rattle's stirring yet —
I like that young Fellow prodigiously — but hold,
I hear him coming — Oh, 'Sdeath it's my damn'd
~~Boxx~~ of a Partner

Enter Tabby. P.S.

Good morrow to you, Sir.

Tabby.

Good morrow! why I am just going to Dinner

Tobine

May be so; but I have scarce breakfasted.

Tabby.

Zounds, I have no patience.

Tobine.

What do you Swear at? What is the matter Mr. Tabby?

Tabby.

Matter? — Do you know, Sir, that a Lady is just gone out of the Shop in a huff, and turn'd four & twenty Yards of Lutestring upon our hands, because you wou'd not go down and speak to her.

Tobine.

I am sorry to hear it, But how can I help her absurdity.

Tabby.
Be civil to all Customers! Keep your Shop and your Shop will keep you! Those were always the Maxims of the Hen and Chickens in your good Old Fathers Time, Mr Tobine.

Tobine.
Very prudent, and provident I cannot dispute.

Tabby.
Cannot dispute! Then why dont you tread in his Footsteps.

Tobine.
Why where's the mighty difference between us.?

Tabby.
No two things in nature more different. Old Humphry Tobine was down Stairs at Seven or Eight by St Pauls Clock every Morning — took a running breakfast — Shaved and dress'd for the Day — and then with a Wig as white as a hoar Frost, and Shoes like jet with the true Patent Blacking, Stood for five or Six Hours bowing to Passengers at the Shop door, Or unrolling Bale, after Bale, with all the Civility,

And

and Small talk imaginable behind the Counter.

Tobine
A very profitable, and pleasant Employment.

Tabby.
Yes, yes, Old Numps minded the main chance. and he had no aversion to pleasure neither. — All his time before Church on a Sunday Morning, he spent making up his Books, in the Compting House   At twelve like a good Christian he brought home the Text — Then he had the whole Day before him — and after Dinner fetch'd a wholesome walk to see his Grandmother at Hampstead and smoked a Comfortable Pipe or two in his way home at Mother Red Caps — There you might have seen him at the Door in his white Night Cap, puff, puff! puff as happy as an Emperor! — The Old Gentlewoman left him a warm Legacy — Ah! honest Numps was the Pride of the Common Council, and I dare say, if he had been alive at this day, would have been an Alderman.

Tobine
But why do you preach this funeral Sermon on my

poor Father to me, M.r Tabby?
Tabby.
Because I wish you your Fathers Son M.r Tobine.
Tobine.
On that Head it wou'd have been more regular in proper time to have Lectur'd my Mother.
Tabby.
Why you young Profligate — Have you no Respect for the Memory of your Parents.
Tobine.
Religious!
Tabby.
Do you make Religion a Jest then? Dead or alive don't you honour your Father, and Mother.
Tobine
The ten Commandments

{ Ranter
{ Catchpenny

Tabby.
Monstrous! There is neither Religion nor Morality among the Young Fellows, now-a-days
Tobine.
Sentimental.
Tabby.

Sentimental! a fine Can't Phrase you have pitch'd upon to laugh at every thing Serious, but have a care, the laugh is not turn'd against you, my Friend! the Contemptible Wretch who attempts to make a Joke of Honour, or Honesty, will find himself the only ridiculous object at last take my Word for it.

Tobine.

Sentimental again! I am surprized you don't write a Comedy Mr. Tabby.

Tabby.

Honesty is the best Policy, Mr. Tobine — Theres another Sentiment for you — a Sentiment that has made the City of London so flourishing — and if any of your Shew folks try to write that old Sterling Sentiment, or any other good Principles out of Countenance, I wish somebody may write their dying Speeches for them. — And so there's another Sentiment — The Gazette comes out twice a Week Remember. — And it is but a short Journey, from Bucklersbury to Guild-hall — but there is such a thing as dissolving Partnership, and Rats will quit a falling House, or a Sinking Ship, and so there's another Sentiment — and so, I wish you a good day Sir. ———————— Exit hastily PS

Tobine
Good day. Old Tabby! — Thus endeth the first Lesson I'd fain begin a new Chapter — It's almost two o'clock, I wonder no-body has call'd — It seems a fine Morning, I'll e'en draw on my Boots, and ride through the new Road to Rotten Row — Sukey Straddle's in the Park, I dare say, in Boots and Spurs, and a pair of Buckskin as Usual — Perhaps she may have another tumble too, and I may be of use to her.

Enter Ranter, & Catchpenny. PS
Ha! Ranter! Catchpenny! My Knights of Adventure Good Morrow! You have pass'd the night, or, rather Morning in the Round House I dare say, what Magician has deliver'd you from the Giants of the Pole, and their Enchanted Castle? — Unfold!

Catchpenny.
You left us in the lurch Squire.

Tobine

Not I faith, honest Catchpenny. My People dragged me into the House, and tost me into Bed — and I was fast asleep before I had time to enquire after you.

Ranter.

Egad little Toby, last nights riot had like to have turn'd out a rehearsal of a Tragedy. They carried us before Old Solomon sitting in Judgment in Guild-hall, and he was going to make us over from the Round House to the Poultry; but it appearing no Windows were broken, but your own, no other harm done, and the Watchmen softned down with a Crown, or two, after a little prosing, as dull as a Sentimental Comedy, he set us at Liberty

Catch.

"Dull as a Sentimental Comedy!" Well said Ranter "Dull as a Sentimental Comedy" Why there is no such thing as a good New Play now, it must be confess'd — but no Wonder Men of Genius are discourag'd from Writing for the

Theatres — Plays are tender Plants, and require the warmth of a Nursery.
Tobine.
Why Modern Plays are apt to be ricketty.
Catch:
The Taste of the Town is depraved, Sir; they relish nothing but Farce, and Outre, and Extravaganza Sir. A Jealous Woman in a Fit, saves one Play from Damnation. calling a whole Family out of their Beds half naked at Midnight is the Salvation of a Second: and the tumbling down of a Screen gives Reputation to another, but they have no true Taste, no damme, no taste after all, for genuine Simplicity, or the Sublime.
Tobine.
Let them feed like the Prodigal upon Husks then! You can supply them with those little Catchpenny
Cathpenny.
Nay, as for that matter, the Town, the Town, are not so much to be blam'd neither. Their Taste is Vitiated by the barbarity and ignorance of the

Managers, and corrupted by the badness of the Actors. If a Poet had the fire of Æschylus in his Composition, the wretched dulness and ignorance of those fellows, wou'd be sure to Extinguish it.

Ranter.

Not so fast, not so fast Master Catchpenny! The present Actors are at least as Excellent as their Authors. Give us a Shakespear, We'll soon produce a Roscius!

Cath.

You grow warm my dear Ranter, sure you cou'd never imagine your_self_ interrested in this Question

Tobine

Oh impossible!

Cath.

No, my dear Ranter, if we had but Six such Actors as _you_, Our Stage would soon Rival the Old famous Performers, Your Betterton's, Your Booth's, and your Garricks, would soon hide their diminished Heads like Stars before the Blaze of the Sun shine.

Ranter.
Oh! my dear Catchpenny!

Cath:
Nay its true — Very true my dear Ranter; I'll be sworn — Is it not Toby?

Tobine.
A mere Truism — no body can dispute it.

Catch.
Besides which, I must say, my dear Ranter, that every time I have seen you lately you seem to have acquired some new excellence — has n't he Toby?

Tobine
Oh yes, always licking up something new like a Snow-ball.

Catch.
Very true! they always speak of Ranter at our Club, by the name of the Theatrical Snowball.

Ranter.

Nay my dear Catchpenny, I no more squinted at You in what I said of the Poets, than you confounded me with the Actors — for Damn me Catchpenny, if I don't think that your Play had Strokes! — Strokes? nay whole Scenes equal to Shakespear. There was a delicacy, a dignity, a — a — you understand me — which I will own many of our Gentlemen were not equal to. I don't care to abuse my profession — but there is scarce an Actor on the Stage, Man, or, Woman that has the least Idea of gesture, or emphasis, Shakespear Otway and Lee, are out of their reach — What Actor Living can speak those Lines.'

"Can none remember." Yes, sure all must.
<u>Tobine</u>.
Well said Ranter.
<u>Ranter</u>.
And then where have you an Actor now equal to the passion of Othello."
"Villain be sure you prove my Love a whore
"Be sure on't! give me Ocular proof.

Catch.
Hold! hold Ranter! this is too violent....
Do you give me that tender speech in the third act of my Play, that you made such a figure in

Ranter.
I'm almost out of breath faith

Tobine.
Nay give us Catchpennys tender Speech, Ranter, – that will be no fatigue to you

Ranter.
I would give it you with all my Heart; but hang me, if I have not entirely forgot it

Tobine.
That's pity.

Catch
Ay, he was not perfect in the piece, when he play'd in it.

Ranter
Not perfect!

Catch.
No, if you had, you wou'd have gain'd such an

Applause in that Speech ———

Ranter.

Applause! why if I remember, that Speech was more hiss'd than any Passage in the whole Play.

Catch.

Yes, your speaking, it, was hiss'd

Ranter.

My Speaking it.

Catch.

I mean your not Speaking it. You were out, and then they hiss'd

Ranter.

No   they hiss'd, and then I was out. Every body allow'd I did the part more than Justice; so don't lay the Damnation of your play upon me.

Catch.

Damnation! what do you mean by Damnation?

Ranter.

Why you know it was acted, but one night

Catch.

No, but it was given out for a Second, after which

my friends left the House — the rest of the Pit and
Galleries were my Enemies — A Set of fellows
that wou'd cut my throat — All Tailors, Sir,
nothing but Tailors.

Ranter

Why should they be angry with you? and how
do you know they were Tailors

Catch.

A friend of mine prov'd it upon them in a Court
of Justice. He prosecuted them for calling them
selves the Town, and convicted them in Westminster
Hall.

Tobine.

A plain case; a Combination of the Journeymen
nothing so evident!

Catch:

Nay, they were wise in not Suffering it to be
Acted again, for the Rascals knew, if it had gone
a Second night, it would have gone fifty.

Ranter.

A thousand, I'll be sworn for it.

Catch.

Not that its fate on the Stage was entirely owing to Enemies neither — for you can't say it had Justice done it by the performers. I am not partial to my own Works, but if ever there was distress in a last Act ——

Ranter.

I am sure the Performers did the Distress of it Justice, for we were pelted with Oranges all the last Act: — We all imagin'd it wou'd be the last Act of our Lives

Catch.

Damnation!

Ranter.

Yes, a Complete Damnation — I told you so —
"For nothing can'st thou to Damnation Add
  Greater than that.

Catch:

Why thou vile retailer of Scraps, fed with the Offals of the Drama — that never knew more of a Play than your own Part, and the Cues that belong'd to it. Do you presume to talk to a Gentleman?

(4) Bounce P.S.

Ranter.

And why not? Sure you forget yourself, Master Catchpenny, Sock and Buskin may hold a Dialogue with Pen and Ink at any Time.

Catch.

Why thou Execrable Barn door Roscius, it is not Seven Years ago, that you and one of the Fifteen miserable Women that bear the Name of Mrs Ranter march'd across the Country with a Jack Ass, and a pair of Paniers; Yourself for want of a Coat in the Habit of Alexander: Statira leading the Ass, with Thunder and Lightning, and other Stage properties in one panier; and a Young Prince of the Blood, and Princess Royal in the Other.

Ranter.

And is it more than three Years ago that you left your Lodgings in the Fleet by favor of an Act of Insolvency? And did not you turn Experimental

Philosopher while you were there.' And did not the People at the Tap refuse to send you Porter, because you melted down the Pewter Pots Rascal.

Tobine.

Nay, but Gentlemen!

Ranter.

And if you talk of Poverty, did not you for many Years live upon Subscriptions for a translation of Hesiod, never intended, nor expected to come out, till you were known all over the Town by the name of Hesiod Catchpenny? — And at last when every body was tir'd out, and your circular Letters of Compliment grown too notorious to raise half a Crown for you — did not your last Wife — for you Beggar, you never could keep above one Wife at a Time — did not your last Wife I say procure a Supply by going about with an Account of your Death, and begging money to bury you.

Tobine.

My dear Ranter! my good friend Catchpenny.

~~Catch.~~

~~I'll trounce in the Green Room him for this.~~

Enter Bounce PS

Tobine.

Oh Bounce, I'm glad to see you Bounce! come and help me to make Peace between these two Gentlemen.

Bounce.

With all my Heart, so you'll assist me in making War afterwards.

Tobine.

War! wheres the Enemy?

Bounce

You Saw how Mr. Squib treated me Yesterday

Tobine

Pshaw! is that all? not less than a dozen Challenges and meetings have past between you and Squib al'ready, and nothing has come of them.

Bounce.

But I have been considering the Affair, and I find, I can't in honour put up with it — I must have him out.

Tobine

Only let him go quietly in again.

Bounce.

I have sent him a Challenge this Morning for Breakfast — Will you be my Second.

Tobine

If you're sure you're in earnest.

Bounce.

I have just bought a new pair of Pistols. May I depend upon you?

Tobine.

Your Time and Place?

Bounce.

The Spa Fields, in a Gravel Pit, within a Stones throw of Islington — about the Dusk of the Evening.

Tobine.

And you're sure you'll do business

Bounce —

His or mine must be done — One of Us must drop I promise you.

Tobine.

Well, then my Friends ⸺⸺⸺ let this fresh Quarrel, that has broken out among other parties be of some use at least, and prove the means of conciliation between you.

Catch.

Nay, I had always the greatest Respect and Regard, for Mr Ranter, and have always said both in Conversation and Print in Theatrical talk and intelligence, he was the most of a Gentleman of any Man in his profession

Ranter.

And I am sure there is not a House about the Garden where I have not constantly Spoke in the highest Terms of Mr Catchpenny, as a Man of Honour and Genius.

Tobine

Well, Buss, and Friends then.

Ranter.
With all my Heart.

Catch:
With the Greatest pleasure

} Both together.

Tobine.

You see Bounce, Squib and you, will come to this presently.

Bounce.

Never, the Spa Fields remember. Blood and Satisfaction The Grave and a Gravil Pit! Good morrow to you.

Tobine.

⟨ Exit. P.S.

Good morrow! Shall we have your Company in the Field Gentlemen?

⟨ Squib P.S.

Ranter.

Why we have a new piece in Rehearsal — I have fail'd several Times, for they make us Rehearse night and Morning: I must shew myself there at least. — So I can't promise you.

Catch.

It is my province as a Poet, and Historian to Record great Actions, but I leave it to such Heroes, as Mr. Bounce, and Mr. Squib to perform them

Tobine.

We shall, meet at Juggins's.

Catch.

Without Doubt.

Ranter.
Most certainly
Catch.
Little Foxy, Good morrow! Come my dear Ranter.
Ranter.
My dear friend Catchpenny.

PS Exeunt Ranter, & Catchp: Embracing
Tobine.
So, the quarrel between Bounce and Squib; and the Reconciliation of Ranter, and Catchpenny are two Events of equal Importance, and in which all the parties are equally in earnest.

Enter Nancy. OP.

Oh! Squire Rattle, good morrow to you! — You stole away last night. What a small Engagement I warrant. I thought you were very sweet on Peggy Williams, young Gentleman.
Nancy.
No faith, I had a Head ache, and came home directly. But I heard you had a riot. You were not hurt I hope?
Tobine.

Tobine

Oh! it's impossible to be hurt, with such prudent Allies as Ranter and Catchpenny, and their Spirit was so little broken by the discipline of the Round house or the Admonitions of the Magistrate that they came to a fresh Rupture this Morning.

Nancy.

Ay, on what Occasion.

Tobine.

The Old Account — themselves to be sure — and before they were reconcil'd. Bounce came with Intelligence of another impending Duel between himself and Squib — Oh, here is Squib; he'll let you know the particulars.

Enter Squib. P.S.

Squib.

Tobine! good day! Dick Rattle, your Servant! Time presses, the Affair is urgent, and I must come to Business immediately — that silly Dog Bounce has sent me a Challenge, and I am to meet him directly

Tobine.

I know it. Bounce has been here just before you

But you'll not fight Squib?
Squib.
Oh! we must fight Sir. There is a silly impertinence about the fellow, that must be Chastis'd. He will never be easy till we have exchang'd Fires.
Tobine.
There has been a deal of Smoke without fire between you hitherto.
Squib.
No doubt of our coming to action at present. I'll make him serious. My Visit was to desire you to accompany me.
Tobine.
I have just engag'd myself to Bounce
Squib
You are a Man of Honour, and I'm glad of it Dick Rattle, here, will go as my Friend.
Nancy.
I— You must Excuse me Mr Squib— I am engag'd on particular business.
Squib.
Zounds, Sir, desert a Man of Honour?

Tobine.
Pshaw! you must go Rattle.
Squib.
To be sure he must. What is your particular Business, to an Affair of this nature, Sir.
Tobine.
Be quiet Squib! Reserve your Fire, till you meet Bounce, Rattle shall attend you, I'll answer for him.
Nancy. (aside)
What can I do!
Squib.
I am satisfied
Nancy.
~~What will become of me~~ (aside)
Tobine.
Away Squib, and prepare the materials. Bounce has told me the Spot and we'll meet you
Squib.
I can Split a Bullet on the Edge of a Penknife
Nancy (aside)
Mercy on me.

Tobine.
Well, well; away and make ready then!
Squib (X'ss)
Bounce is a dead Man,. I can hit a Sixpence or a Waistcoat Button, not broader than a Marrow =fat at twenty Yards. distance — a dead man, damme. ——— Exit P.S.

Manet Tobine & Nancy.
Tobine.
Ha! ha! I am half angry with you, Rattle, I know you dispise these Reptiles as much as I do. when a Joke is so ripe, how cou'd you think of foregoing it?

Nancy.
I have no objection to a Joke; but a Duel is a very Serious Affair.

Tobine.
A very ridiculous Affair between such parties I promise you. We must punish their mock Valour, for its impertinence

Nancy.
You may if you please — but I had rather.——

<u>Tobine</u>
Why sure you are not afraid Rattle?
<u>Nancy.</u>
No, no; not afraid — but — but —
<u>Tobine.</u>
Nay, if you were it wou'd not Signify — do but keep your own Counsel. A Child with a Wooden Gun would over match both of them. We'll cool their Courage for the future I warrant you.
<u>Nancy</u>
Well, I shall Submit to your direction — But I am glad to see you in such Spirits, and hope they proceed from your having drop't the dreadful thoughts you hinted to me.
<u>Tobine</u>
Just the Contrary: They rather prove my having made up my mind, Rattle — My Affairs are come to a Crisis, and most damnably entangled they are to be sure — I must cut the Knot — there's no untying
<u>Nancy.</u>
You make me Shudder to mention it; and your chear

=fullness in a State so desperate. —
Tobine.
Oh! nothing so easy, as a Man in despair.
Nancy.
I always thought otherwise
Tobine.
In Books, Poems, Plays, Novels, and Romances, I grant you — But not in real Life; not in the World — Do but look at all the People that are Ruin'd without Resource, and see how easy they are! Hope! hope! is a State of Anxiety, I grant you. Fear and Suspense are distraction, but once plunge into the Gulph of Despair, your Cares are Swallow'd up in an Instant.
Nancy.
But I see no necessity for your plunging into it Your affairs are not so desperate.
Tobine.
What wou'd you have me go out in a Smother? Stick my Life upon a Save-all, or glimmer in the Socket? No, I'll clap on the Extinguisher

while I am in full Blaze my Boy.
Nancy.
But for a Man scarce involved in any difficulties, not encumber'd with Debts. —
Tobine.
There's my Comfort Rattle. I have run out my own Fortune to be sure, and my last Guinea, and last Moment will come pretty nearly together, but I Scorn to hurt any body else. The World shall see, when I wind up the Account that I have involv'd no Partners, taken in no friends, deserted no Bondsmen, and forfeited no Securities; I am partial to men of pleasure, and people of Fashion to be sure, but damn me if I have not been Surpriz'd how some of them cou'd go off in peace when they only finish'd themselves at home, after Actions for which they ought rather to have been finish'd at Tyburn.
Nancy.
Your way of thinking is noble, but still rather too Violent. You once told me of an Opening to

settle yourself advantageously in marriage.

Tobine.

Why that at first sight appears the least desperate measure of the two; and there is a generous Girl who I know was partial enough to me, to have taken me, such as I am for better, for worse. but I could not trust my own Passions or her power far enough to be convinc'd of Stopping in my Career; So I rather chose to abide the issue alone than incur the Chance of involving her I lov'd — for I did love her Rattle — and her that lov'd me in my indiscretions.

Nancy

Sure it is not even yet too late to apply to her.

Tobine.

No, no; I have rather us'd her ill, and can't submit to Confession, penance and mortification — No, I'm resolv'd to go — in my circumstances it is Spirited, honourable, and genteel — the Die is Cast, the Game is up — all I am in doubt about is the mode of effecting it — What d'ye think of a Pistol.

Nancy.

Shocking! to be shot like a Deserter! It is too much in the Stile of a common Malefactor.

Tobine

Why that was my Objection to hanging! tho' I attended three Executions on purpose to see the Effects of it. I have had some thoughts of drowning I am told it is not unpleasant.

Nancy.

Had not you better only report you are drown'd?

Tobine.

Report I am drowned! what good will that do me?

Nancy.

Oh! a great deal — First of all, we can insure twenty or thirty thousand on your Life; then advertize a reward to the Bargemen, and Lightermen, for the Body of a Gentleman who walk'd out towards Black Friars or Westminster Bridge; and then, on your non-appearance; conclude you lost in the Thames, and come upon the underwriters.

Tobine.
You jest Rattle — You know I have too much honour, Sink, or Swim, I'll not be a Scoundrel.
Nancy.
Drowning will not do at any rate
Tobine
Why not?
Nancy.
The contemptible Exit of Kittens & blind puppies Besides it's impossible.
Tobine
Impossible!
Nancy.
Absolutely. They'll take you up, and bring you to Life again.
Tobine.
That's damn'd hard, in a free Country; I did not think of that. Drowning will not do then. What would you advise me to Rattle?
Nancy.
Will you leave the Management of this Matter to me.

Tobine.

Implicitly, there is a softness, and Sensibility, a good nature, and integrity about you that have taken me, wonderfully, or I should not have let you far into my Confidence, It is only for you and a few more of your Complexion, that Life is worth a moments reflection — But a Short Life and a merry one — that has been always my Maxim Rattle — So what is your Counsel.'

Nancy.

Why if it must be so — my prescription, is poison

Tobine

So are many other prescriptions — But why Poison?

Nancy.

A gentle Opiate, I mean, a mere Anodyne, for I would have your End as easy as your Life has been Jovial.

Tobine

I like your Idea — and will you undertake to purchase the Cordial.

Nancy.

I will provided you will Solemnly engage yourself to use no other means till you have tried the effect of it.

Tobine

I will not upon my Honour, when I have said that you know you may trust me.

Nancy.

I am sure of it — and you shall find me equally faithfull. but still I hope you will alter your mind, when you have got over this fit of melancholy.

Tobine. {Ring}

No Melancholy in the Case my friend, the Spleen, and the Climate are mere common place notions, and totally groundless; Gentlemen end themselves only because they can't live any longer. High living, and not low Spirits, is the Phisical cause of their Conduct, fine Houses, fine Girls, and fine Horses have fifty times the influence of a gloomy November.

Nancy.

I believe you are a good deal in the Right

but have you no Apprehensions.
Tobine.
Oh! I guess what you mean. None at all. Some books I read while I sat under my Hair Dresser, have made me quite easy on those Subjects
Nancy
And to what wise Philosophers, is the inside of your Head indebted for such Signal Obligations
Tobine.
To a couple of Doctors, very deep reasoners I assure you, Read the Calculations and thoughts of One Doctor, and the Disquisitions of another; Take your Ideas of civil Liberty from the first, and your notions of Philosophical necessity, from the Second; and you make yourself perfectly easy about Religion, or Politicks. One will convince you that the nation like individuals will be announced Bankrupt in the Gazette in less than a twelvemonth, and the other will prove as plain as a pike Staff, that Matter and Spirit, Soul and body, are both the same thing, both lighted up

and Extinguish'd at the very same instant.
Such Authors make us quite careless about
our fortunes, or Actions here, and totally
indifferent as to the fate or event of hereafter.
                              Exit. O P.

           End of Act 2d.
                              Drop Saloon

Act 3do

(1) Globe Flat 1G (1) ~~Drams Cloth~~

D:Truby } OP *An apartment at D:Truby's.*
Nancy }

Enter D:^{r} Truby and Nancy. OP.

Truby.
And your Suspisions really prove true then?

Nancy.
Too true, Sir

Truby.
So that what he threw out carelessly, turns out to be his serious intention.

Nancy.
Most Serious.

Truby.
I always said, he was a Blockhead – an ignorant

Nancy.
Believe me my dear Doctor Truby, you mistake his Character.

Truby.
Ay, you are as great a Fool as He. or, you wou'd not be so partial to him.

Nancy.

He has indeed an unhappy turn for pleasure and a silly Ambition of being a fine Gentleman. but yet ——

Truby.

A fine Gentleman, I never knew any good come of your fine Gentlemen, especially of your City fine Gentlemen. The Red Heels to their Shoes and White Feathers in their Hats, may serve well enough, to shew the lightness, and Emptiness of the proud Monkies at the West End of the Town; but a Citizen, should from Head to foot be a Citizen. There is a certain Solid Dignity, a heavy Grandeur about the Mansion House that becomes the Top of Cheapside. A Change Alley Broker, a Lombard Street Clerk, or a Ludgate Hill Mercer turn'd Fop and Macaroni, ridiculous, and as much out of Character as if the Giants at Guildhall were seen dancing a Minuet at Almacks, or the Pantheon.

Nancy.

But some Allowance, Sir, must surely be made for his Youth, and then ill chosen Company —

Truby.

Company ill chosen with a Witness! the highest of the low, and the lowest of the high — Ah! I knew no good wou'd come of it, when he got acquainted with Lord what d'ye call him. — took him up two pair of Stairs into his Phaeton, and carried him out of Town on parties of Pleasure with his Lordships led Captains and kept Mistresses.

Nancy.

Truce with your Satire my dear Doctor, have some pity for me at least, and think what I must Suffer at the present moment.

Truby.

Why I do pity you, and that's the Reason I abuse the Puppy, and I would not abuse him if I had not a Regard for him — The nonsense of the rest of the young Blockheads about Town never disturbs me.

Nancy.
But my dear Doctor Truby, you are my Confident consider, and ought to comfort me.
Truby.
Yes, you are a Female Quixote, and I am your Medical Sancho; an Old Fool, that sees all your Follies, and yet assists you in the pursuit of them.

(2)
Tobine
Bounce

Nancy.
Do but bring this Adventure to a happy conclusion, and it shall be our last Sally Doctor
Truby
Don't be too confident of success. The Damn'd Windmill Vertigo of Dissipation has kept such a Whirl in his Ideas, that it has turn'd his brain.
Nancy.
His Principles are sound, I am sure; and you know the Heart often corrects the Head Doctor.
Truby.

Where it does not, the Heart and Head I know are both good for nothing

Nancy.

Bring him to a thorough Sense of his Extravagancies, and I am persuaded he will abandon them — but where is this Potion Doctor? I am terrified at the very Idea. tho' I know that you'll give him nothing that is not perfectly harmless.

Truby.

He'll not think it so, I promise you. The preparation is innocent enough in its Consequences it is true, but it is likely to give him some very Serious alarms in the Course of its operation.

Nancy.

But if those Alarms, Doctor. —

Truby.

Nay, if you deliver him from his apprehensions too soon, you will not only betray me, but most probably restore him to his Absurdities. we must purge his Passions, by means of Pity, and Terror, like the old Writers of Tragedy. A thin, Water gruel Composition that is not strongly impregnated with both, is not worth a Farthing

<u>Nancy.</u>
Sweeten his Blood and correct his humours with whatever Decoction you please Doctor.

<u>Truby.</u>
Nothing more bracing than Bitters, no Alterative more effectual than Wormwood — Come with me, and I'll furnish you immediately — but be sure to act as I order you.

<u>Nancy.</u>
I'll administer nothing without your direction, or consent, depend on it.

<u>Truby.</u>
And what a pretty Use you make of your Physician Madam.

<u>Nancy</u>
The best in the World Doctor, no Practice was

ever half so Beneficial.

Truby.

Beneficial! why I shall be paragraph'd with the compleat Virmin killer, advertiz'd for in Journals, and Mercury's, to dose Ferrets Foxes, and Polecats, and cried at Wakes and Fairs, as a Fellow that Travels the Country with Quicksilver, Arsenick, and Ratsbane — nay perhaps I may be known all over the Town in a Fortnight, by the Nick name of Romeo's Apothecary   Exeunt OP.

Wing Bell. ⎫
nd Whistle ⎭ @ Scene Spa Fields 2)
                 Open Country.

Enter Tobine & Bounce PS.

Bounce (Singing)

"Dragons, pour, boine, on dit give vous avez le mon — um — um — um — a fine afternoon Mr. Tobine. um! — um! —

Tobine.

Very fine, and very pleasant.

Bounce   {(3) Squib / Nancy} PS

Oh! Extreamly pleasant.
Mais poure combattre On dit que nom, um! um!

Tobine.

Why you're in Spirits Bounce:

Bounce.

Pretty well, Sir! — But Sir, I always hum a tune when I am serious, Sir. — One of the old Philosophers always repeated his A. B. C when he was in a Passion, Sir; and a late Nobleman who knew the World better than any body, always advises to do every thing in Minuet Time, Sir — Dragons pour boine &c. How do you like these Pistols Mr Tobine? handsomely Mounted, Rifle Barrell'd you see. . On dit que vous etez.

Tobine

Rifle Barrell'd — have a care Bounce; You may kill two Birds with One Stone perhaps.

Bounce.

Sir, I don't desire to kill any body, Sir.

I have been unlucky enough to be often involv'd in quarrels, but I am a Man of a very peaceable disposition, I assure you, Sir. —
Ni de coup de Sabre.

Tobine.

We are first on the Ground, Bounce, can we derive any Advantage from it?

Bounce.

None at all, Sir. Ni de pistolet.

Tobine.

The last Time you call'd Squib out, I am told you were at the Spot, an hour before the time, he came an Hour after the Time, and so you never met at all.

Bounce.

Sir, it was partly to rectify that mistake, I, appointed him now, Sir.

Tobine.

He makes it very late tho' — if he should not come at all.

Bounce.

To be sure, I have heard of Cowardly Poltroons, fellows that.
Tobine.
Ha! here he comes: Squib, and Dick Rattle with him.
Bounce.
Yes, yes, I know Mr. Squib would be punctual a Man of Honour and Courage, Sir. Dragons, pour boire &c. S.

Enter Squib & Nancy. PS
Tobine.
Oh! your Servant Gentlemen! Come, we have no Time to lose, let's to business immediately, the Pops are much of a Length I hope. Where are yours Bounce?
Bounce.
Here, Sir, are my Instruments — um — um —
Tobine.
And yours Squib.
Squib.
Here! high-ho!

Tobine.

All fair well how far will you stand?
not less than ten paces I hope; Let me see

Nancy.

Stay, Sir; just before we arriv'd, Mr Squib said
something of an Accommodation.

Tobine.

Accommodation? impossible. Rattle you know
to what length matters have been carried between
them.

Bounce.

Let's hear what the Gentleman has to say, however,
Mr Tobine.

Squib.

Nay, I only said, that Mr Bounce to be sure had
a right to demand the Satisfaction of a Gentleman
if he thought himself affronted to be sure;
but I declare upon my Honour that I never
meant any affront to him.

Bounce.

No, did not you mean to Sneer at my Affair, with

Bounce.

To be sure — if you supposed that I glanc'd at you it is no wonder that you should allude to me. But I declare to you M^r. Squib, and to these Gentlemen here, that I had no such intention

Squib.

No.

Bounce.

No, upon my honour, Sir

} 4 Juggins
4 Waiters

Squib.

Why then if you meant no reflection upon me; I am very ready to make a proper apology; for any Chance Words that might be offensive to you

Bounce

Why, Sir; if you are willing to acknowledge.

Tobine.
Oh! damn me! they are come to their *Ifs* again. Hark ye. Gentlemen, if you meant an Explanation You shou'd have thought of it before, Are we to be made fools every time you choose to expose yourselves?

Squib.
Why, Sir, if we are both Satisfied, no offence was intended on either side,, and if——

Tobine.
Ay, more *Ifs* — these are a couple of Scoundrels Lets Kick them Rattle.

Nancy.
Lord, Sir, I came here as Mr Squibs friend — consider.

Tobine.
Well then not to fail in point of good Manners, I will kick your Friend, and you shall kick mine if you please.

~~Bounce~~

~~But Sir.~~

Squib.
But Mr. Tobine.
Nancy.
~~I'm sure you'll excuse me.~~ o. t. i.
Tobine.
Nay I insist upon it. And first of all, here goes for Example...
Squib.
Mighty fine, Sir. I shall remember this?
Tobine.
I hope you'll never forget it — now your Foot to my Friend, Rattle.
Nancy.
I beg your Pardon Mr. Bounce, but you see it is not in my power to Act Otherwise ... you'll Excuse me, Sir.
Bounce.
I shall pardon you, Sir, for your politeness, & civility but we are not amply reveng'd on your Friend there G. J v th Sj b
Tobine.

<u>Tobine</u>.

Hold Gentlemen, before you go, One Word more with you to put an entire Stop to your Vapouring and Challenges for the future, I will have you confess plainly, that you are both Scoundrels and Cowards.

<u>Squib</u>.

Well, you are pleas'd to say so, Sir.

<u>Tobine</u>.

Say it yourselves, Rascals! and Bounce you shall be Spokesman.

<u>Bounce</u>.

Very well — Suppose us so, if you please, Sir.

<u>Tobine</u>.

Suppose won't do, I must have it from your own Mouth, Sir.

<u>Bounce</u>.

Well, you have, Sir

<u>Tobine</u>.

In so many Words, Sir.

<u>Bounce</u>..

Tobine.
Kick him again Rattle
Nancy.
I beg your pardon, Sir ~~the officer...~~
Bounce.
Zounds what wou'd you have?
Tobine.
I wou'd have you declare in express Terms, that you and Squib are a Couple of Cowards and Scoundrels.
Bounce.
Well, to oblige you, Sir. we are Cowards, and Scoundrels.
Tobine (to Squib.)
Echo him Sirrah.
Squib.
Oh, yes, we are Scoundrels, and Cowards to be sure, Mr Bounce
Tobine.
Once more Salute, my Friend, Master Deputy.
(Nancy kicks out Bounce

Tobine

and here take your own friend, at the rebound
like a Tennis Ball {Kicks Sq overts away. to
(P.S.)

So much for an Affair of Honour! and now Rattle
for our Party at Juggins's, and as we go we'll
confer upon Business.

Nancy.

Oh, my dear Friend, do but reflect.

Tobine.

If you love me Rattle, don't talk of Reflection.
of all Things in nature it is the most insupportable

{Wing Bell}   Exeunt P.S.
{Whistle}   Scene the Tavern. {Table
            Globe Flatt.   4 Chairs.

Enter Juggins & Waiters O.P.

Juggins.

Come bustle, bustle, get this Room Ready for M.r Tobine
and his Company — quick, quick — they'll be here
presently — and you know he always chuses the
Mermaid — The Room smells of Tobacco like a

Hackney Writers eating House, or, an Inn at the University

Robin 1.st Waiter.

The Gentlemen that dined here, are but just gone Sir.

Juggins.

How the Devil came you to shew them in here; a Set of Stupid Fellows, muddling for four Hours over their Ink Bottles of thick Port, and then Casting up the Bill, and paying their Reckoning by Items, so, that one can't mount an odd five Shillings, or Squeeze in an Extra Article Edgways.

Antony 2.d Waiter.

And then not leaving above half a Crown for the Waiter — Zounds, a Man might as well be a worsted Stocking Parson, or a half pay Officer as a genteel Waiter at that rate

Juggins.

Oh! you think of yourselves, but never consider your Master.

1st Waiter. Robin.

Indeed we do, Sir. To pluck the Guests and to feather your Nest, is all our Study, Sir.

Juggins.

That's an honest Lad .. Those are the right principles of a thorough good Servant. — A very honest Lad, but harkee, Robin.

1st Waiter Robin

Sir!

Juggins.

How came you to let Mr. Tobine have the Claret with the Anchor and black Seal, all Yesterday Evening.

1st Waiter. Robin

You know it's the Sort he likes, and he is one of those you always wish to oblige, Sir.

Juggins.

Yes, for the first three or four Bottles — but you shou'd have chang'd it upon them afterwards — It's all one by that time — At least you may swear them out of the difference.

1st Waiter. Robin

I'll take care for the future, Sir.
Juggins.
Do so, always mind your Business, and be true
to your Master — You, Antony.   (5)
2.d Waiter Antony
{ Tobine
Ranter
Nancy
Catchpenn.
Sir.
Juggins.
How came you not to Charge Harriet Spriggens's,
Chair hire, in the reckoning last night?
2.d Waiter Antony
She came afoot, Sir.
Juggins
Foot — You Greenhorn! and what then, Sir.
2.d Waiter. Antony
Nay it was not only for that, Sir: but you know
She lives but at next door.
Juggins.
And suppose, she liv'd in the House, Sir, what's
that to the purpose? You should always charge
Coach or Chair hire, if it was but for the Honour
of the Lady, and the credit of the Garden, You
Blockhead. why you may as well bring a Lady

in Pattens. (Ready o R 13

2ᵈ Waiter. Antony
I'll make up for it another time, Sir.

Juggins.
See you do then, never wrong the House, Remember that's the way to be known for an honest Servant and to keep up a good Character. Tom Cellerman!

Tom 3ᵈ Waiter.
Sir.

Juggins.
Have you got in the Vitrol to quicken the Claret

Tom 3ᵈ Waiter.
I have, Sir.

Juggins.
And the Turnips for the Champagne!

Tom 3ᵈ Waiter.
Yes, Sir.

Juggins.
And the black Currants to brew the old Port.

Tom 3ᵈ Waiter.
Yes, Sir.

Juggins

And is the Poker in the Fire, to make the Spa, Water?

Tom 3ᵈ *Waiter.*

All ready, Sir.   (Bar Bell Rings)

Juggins.

Oh! I hear the Gentlemen coming — now be sure you open Bottles of as many different Wines as possible during Supper time.

Robin 1ˢᵗ *Waiter.*

We shall, Sir.

Juggins

And when the Cloth's taken away, put on Olives, and, Pistachia Nuts. and so forth, call'd for, or not call'd for, d'ye hear?

Tom 3ᵈ *Waiter.*

Very well, Sir.

Juggins.

And plates of Dutch Beef, and Anchovies on Toast about two in the Morning.

Robin 1ˢᵗ *Waiter.*

To be sure, Sir.

Juggins.

<u>2^d Waiter.</u>
We'll take care, Sir.
<u>Juggins.</u>
Do so, do so; never neglect any Articles, that may run up the Reckoning. Twist, Staytape, and Buckram — make out the Bill remember.
<u>1st Waiter.</u>
We'll be sure to do you Justice, Sir.
<u>Juggins.</u>
Ay, ay, never wrong the House, and by, and by you may come to have honest Servants under you and keep a House yourselves perhaps — Stand clear, here come the Gentlemen.
<u>Enter Tobine, Ranter, Catchpenny &c. P.S.</u>
<u>Chairs pro O.v.</u>
Light those Candles Robin; bring up the Wine Antony
<u>Tobine.</u>
Some of your Old Brandy, first Juggins.
<u>Exit Juggins O.P.</u>

Zounds I'm as cold with the Air of the Spa Fields as if I'd been up to the Chin in the New River. the Rascals. were oblig'd to us for Kicking them Ranter -if it was only for the sake of warming them

Ranter.

It must have been a pleasant Scene, I wish I had been there.

Catch

I shall take the hint, and Advertize the Duellists. a Satire, immediately.

Ranter.

And may your Satire produce as good a Bottle and Bowl as this here before us Catchpenny.

Catch.

Well said Ranter — Come little Toby.

Tobine.   {All Seat themselves

Zounds! I'm frozen; where is this Brandy.

Enter Juggins.

Here, Sir! right Nantz — genuine French Spirit as ever was Tasted.   _Helps Tobine_

Tobine.

Give me another Glass. — Here goes — now I'm primed — so lets to Business. {Going towards the Table Sir.

Juggins.

Here is the Change out of the Thirty pound Note your Honour, left with me to discharge the Marshalsea Writ, for Miss Judy Atkinson. The Debt and Costs — came to nine pounds twelve, Sir.

Tobine.

Give poor Judy the rest then! and tell her to buy Mourning with it, for the first Friend she loses. (Goes to the Table

Juggins. {Waiter with Decanter}

I shall, Sir; this Mourning will make her quite joyfull.   Exit O P.

Tobine.

Well, said my Boys; Come, here's a Bumper, much good may do you, my Bucks.

Catch.

Come Gentlemen, a general Hob-nob, to little Toby's good Health. ___ (All Drink)

Tobine.

A Glass of thanks my Boys! And now we have all whet our Whistles, let's have your last Prize Catch Ranter.

Ranter.

With all my heart. Toby! Strike up, and mind your hits my Boys.——

A Catch.

Twas you Sir.
Twas you, Sir.

Catchpenny.

Brava! — Bravissimo! we begin to wax jolly now — What d'ye say, shall we have the Wenches up Toby?

Tobine.

Pshaw! no.

Catch.

And why not Toby?

Tobine.

Prithee be quiet and Toy with your Imagination for this Evening Catchpenny. Come, Charge, and Drink about my Boys..

Catch. (apart to Ranter.)

What a queer humour he is in. If he won't allow us the Girls; lets have some Hazard Ranter.

Ranter.

I'll give a broad hint — um — um — Zounds, this Table's full of Dents from the Dice Box, as Pat Johnsons Face from the Small Pox. — Suppose we call for the Tatts — and have a merry Main — Eh! Toby?

Tobine.

Damn your Main, what should we play for? I have no money to lose, and I am sure you have none for me to win. Ranter, drink about, I say

Catch.

So he has nick'd you, Ranter.

Ranter.

The Squire is in a droll Vein indeed to-night.

Tobine.

Come, here goes, another Catch and a half-pint my Bucks.

Ranter.

No, no; we'll have a Glee; We'll Sing Old Rose

and burn the Bellows.

Catch.
Old Rose and burn the Bellows.

Tobine.   (Ring.)
Well done, well done! Sung like any nightingale
Come, one more round my Lads and then.
Bonus nocius.

Catch:
Bonus nocius! what d'ye mean Toby.

Tobine.
Mean! I thought you were a Scholar Catchpenny
Bonus nocius, is Latin for good night you know

Ranter.
Good night? why we are scarce warm in our
Chairs yet.

Tobine.
No matter for that, I have business, so good night
I say. the dearest Friends must part, so good
night I say again — We are at the last Page.
Finis, Catchpenny, — The Play's over, Ranter
Exeunt Omnes, so away with you — I pay the

Reckoning, you know, so away with you —
Enter Waiter.
Here Waiter, bring me a Pint of Brandy, and take away the Gentlemen.

Catchpenny.
This is the strangest Whim.

Ranter.
Well, good night Toby! You'll hear of us at the Piazza, when you come to yourself again

Tobine.
Very well, — You'll hear of me presently (*Exeunt PS*

Tobine. (Solus)
Enter Waiter with Brandy.

So, now I'm alone.
One Charge more.
     "If thus a Man can die
         "Much bolder with Brandy. (*half Singing*)
Much Virtue in good Brandy, to be sure —
But let me see — To be, or not to be, that is the question
To be a Gentleman, a Man of the World, a Man of Property, a Man of Pleasure — 'Tis a Situation devoutly to be wish'd — But then to be ruin'd.

to be a Bankrupt, to be in the Gazette, Ay there's the Rub. <u>Come Cordial, and not Poison</u> <u>taking o a Phial</u> But hold! <u>what if this Mixture do not Work at all</u> Why suppose it should not, I am but where I was, only that I shall be oblig'd to call Rattle to account, for cheating me.

"And yet methinks he should not
"For he hath still been tried an honest fellow. Here's to his Health — and here's to my true Love, my dear Nancy Lovell too (*drinks*) <u>Oh! potent draught</u> Whether it is the potion, or the Wine, and the Brandy Whether, I have drank myself dead, or am dead Drunk, I can't tell — but I feel cursed Sick, and very heavy to sleep, and woe! woe! be to Dick Rattle, if I ever wake again.

<u>Sleeps & the Curtain Drops.</u>

<u>End of Act the Third.</u>   (25 Minutes)
        <u>Speak to give out the Play.</u>
     <u>Nancy to Dress.</u>

Enter Juggins & Waiters OP

Juggins.

Sent for to Mr. Tibines, what is it over with him then?

1st Waiter.

Not quite, Sir; but so bad it seems that he is not expected to recover —

Juggins

But how came we to be sent for. {John. (2) Peggy}

2d Waiter.

By Order of Squire Ferret, his Worship from the Rotation Office, who is now attending to take our Examination, and has summoned us before the whole Bench in Bow Street to-morrow.

Juggins.

Why so?

1st Waiter.

Because they say the Squire was poison'd by the

Juggins.
The Wine! Oh! the Devil! Tom Cellarman.
3d. Waiter
Sir

Juggins.
You certainly put too much Arsenick into that Madeira. you dog.
3d. Waiter
Not more than usual, I assure you, Sir.
Juggins.
Come, come, I know it was foul, when it came from the Minories — Confess, did it not want help a little.
3d. Waiter.
Not in the least Sir
Juggins.
Did not you put him into the Chair, Antony.
2d. Waiter.
I did, Sir, Robin, and I brought him down Stairs, and pack'd him off together, Sir.

1.st Waiter.

He neither mov'd, nor stirr'd Sir. and whether he was dead, or in Liquor, or asleep, we could not tell, Sir.

Juggins.

But.

Juggins.

Are you sure there was a Phial found in the Room, where Mr Tobine spent the Evening

2.^d Waiter.

Quite, Sure, — here it is, Sir.

Juggins.

Well, well, you're an honest Lad and I know you'll say so, for the good of the House But—

2.^d Waiter.

Say so — I'll Swear it.

Juggins.

Yes, for the good of the House, I know you

but we are only friends here, so now you may Speak Truth; was this little Phial really found there.

2ᵈ Waiter.

It was indeed, Sir. just as you see it, on the Floor, Sir.

Juggings.

What no little paper Cravat with a direction upon it?

(3) John Bolus

2ᵈ Waiter.

None at all, Sir.

Juggings

Faugh how it smells — Here take it again Robin and be sure you Stick to your Text now.

2ᵈ Waiter.

I warrant you, Sir.

Juggins.

And Tom Cellarman, not a word of the Arsenick, d'ye hear.

2ᵈ Waiter.

Not a Syllable Sir — I'd no more betray the

Secrets of Trade, than take a true Oath at the Custom House.

Juggins.

Thats an honest Fellow: always the good of the House remember! Ah! I never thought my old Friend Mr Tobine would have serv'd me so a Stranger indeed! — I shou'd not have wonder'd but for a friend to take away the Credit of the House by coming here to destroy himself — It was very unkind of him — But come along. — Sink the Arsenick! and stick to the Phial — Came along, Boys.   { Exeunt PS } { (4) Peggy }

An Apartment at Tobines. ②
1st Chamber no Change of Wings
Bell Rings violently. Enter hastily
John & Peggy meeting
Peggy with Jugs, Mugs, Basons &c.

John.

Oh! here Peggy give me those Rings — I'll take them to my Masters Room, and do you run for some

more Carduus, and Camomile Flowers immediately
and send up some more Mugs, and Pans, and
Basons immediately

(5)
{ Ranter
{ Catchpeny

Peggy.   John.
I will and get a Flask of Florence Oil —
    Peggy.
but how is my Master John?   (Bell ready)

John.
Very bad, very bad indeed

Peggy.
Poor dear Gentleman, oh la! what shall we do
for him   Exeunt Severally.

                                    Bell rings
                            PS
Re Enter John. hastily meeting Bolus the Apothecary

John.
Here bring the — Oh Mr. Bolus, I am glad you are
come back, I was just going to send for you.

Bolus.
How is the Patient.

John.
Worse, and worse I think, Sir.

Bolus.

(6)
{ Dr Truby } Bell
{ Tabby   } ready
{ Mrs Grogram
{ Nancy

Small Bell PS

Has Doctor Truby been here, yet?

John.

No, Sir; he was sent for out of Town to Lord Flimseys early this Morning, but is expected home every instant.

Enter Peggy running PS

Peggy.

Here are the basons, and the Cloths, and the

John.

Run up with them directly then.

Peggy.

I fly. — Oh dear me — *Exit Peggy OP.*

John.

Up those Stairs — You know the way, Sir.

Bolus. (going) (returns.)

He's not asleep I hope.

John.

Broad awake, but in great pain, Sir.

Bolus.

So much the better — Did they give him the Chalk Emulsion, I order'd him, every half hour.

John.
They did, Sir.
Bolus.
And have they put on the Blisters to the Soles of his Feet?
John.
Yes, Sir.
Bolus.
And chaf'd his Temples, and burnt Brimstone under his Nose.
John
Ale, Sir.
Bolus.
Oh! very well. ——— (Ex~~it~~ ~~severally~~)

Enter Ranter & Catchpenny.
Catch.
Oh! here is his Man, he can inform us.
Ranter.
How is your Master John?
John.
Exceedingly ill, Sir.

Catch.
We are very sorry for it, But is his illness owing to the Wine he drank last night John?

John.
Something he had at the Tavern no doubt, Sir.

Ranter.
I thought so — I said it had a damn'd Taste. And the Punch was a Bowl of Poison

Catch.
I turn'd Sick, the moment I got up this Morning Zounds, I shan't be easy this twelvemonth

Ranter.
Can't we see your Master

John
By, and bye, Sir; please to Step into the next Room, Sir. <u>Exit John. OP.</u>

Ranter.
We will — I'm in a cold Sweat.

Catch.
I'm in a burning Fever.

Ranter.

Ranter.

Zounds Catchpenny what a Catastrophe

Catchp.

My dear Ranter what a Figure this will cut in the news papers. —

Enter Dr Fruby. Tabby, Mrs Groggram and Nancy in Womans Cloaths UP.

Tabby.

We are very much oblig'd to Dr Fruby to be sure but this is a Touch of the Times: this comes of his wanting to be a Gentleman. Till within these Seven Years. I never heard of an Attempt of the kind on this side of Temple Bar, since I have been in business

Mrs Grog.

No truly; it is enough for your Lords and Dukes and your Quality at the other End of the Town to hang and Drown, and Shoot themselves a Sober Citizen never us'd to hurt himself, or, his Family, however he might make free with other people.

Dr. Truby.

Well, my good Friends, the secret you are now made acquainted with is the best apology for the late Conduct and disguise of your Kinswoman and if we manage him properly, in his present Situation, perhaps we shall be able to insure the future happiness of your Family, give peace and quiet to this Girl, who is fool enough to doat on him, and not only restore the blockhead himself to the World, but make him a Valuable Member of Society.

Tabby.

Why to be sure, if he would but have given his mind to Business, no-body had a better notion of it — Ten times cleverer than old Numps, (7) that I must say for him.

PS { Servant / Handbill / Wingrave

Dr. Truby.

How was he, when you left him Madam.

Mrs Grod.

In a peck of troubles poor Soul! So Sick, and so miserable, so sure of being at Death's door.

as he thinks, and yet so desirous to live, it wou'd make your Heart yearn again.

Nancy.

Indeed my dear Dr Truby, I begin to dread the Consequences of what he has taken, the agitation of his mind is of itself sufficient to be fatal to him.

Dr Truby.

Not a bit I tell you; his mind must be agitated still more, and if you don't follow my prescription in this Case, I'll give you over forever.

Nancy.

I shall certainly continue to be govern'd by you, Sir, but———

Dr Truby.

As to what he has taken, don't be uneasy about that, however alarm'd, he is in no sort of Danger. I promise you — We have frighten'd him with the apprehensions of death already, and if the fellow has as much principle, as I always thought he had, we shall inspire him with the most anxious desire of Life again.

<u>Nancy.</u>
Pray Heaven we may.
<u>Dr Truby.</u>
Does he know of your being here?
<u>Mrs Grog.</u>
Yes, that he does, he has ask'd after her a hundred, and a hundred times over, and raves about Nancy Lovell, and his Dear Friend Dick Rattle.
<u>Dr Truby.</u>
We must interest him stile more for both these Characters — You may Visit him now — we'll follow you presently — hay keep up your Spirits, and go thro' with the business, you play'd the Man's part to a Miracle, but you'll spoil all if you put on too much softness with your Petticoats. Reserve your Tenderness for a proper Occasion.
<u>Nancy.</u>
I'll do all in my power, Sir. (Exit Weeping)
<u>Dr Truby.</u>
'Psha! the Girls a Natural, and yet her Sorrow

will answer our purpose well enough. if she does not betray us: We had better not leave her too long, alone with him. (going OP) ─────

    Enter Servant. PS.
   Servant (to Tabby)

Mr Wingrave desires to speak to you, Sir.
    Tabby.

Wingrave! who's he! — what does he want?
    Servant.

Lives in Cheapside, Sir; and has sent in One of his Shop Bills ─── ── (Gives Bill)
    Tabby.

Well, desire him to walk up then. { Exit Serv.ᵗ } PS
    Dr Truby.

Come Madam, we'll visit our patient, and leave Mr Tabby to his business.
    Exeunt Dr Truby & Mrs Grog: OP.
    Tabby.

"What have we here (reading) "Peter Wingrave" "Upholsterer, Appraiser, Undertaker, and Auctioneer "Furnishes Funerals"! What the Plague does the fellow
            want

Wing.
Your very humble Servant, Sir.
Tabby.
And what is your pleasure with me, Sir?
Wing.
I came, Sir, in hopes of your Commands for your Partner's Funeral.
Tabby.
Funeral.
Wing.
Yes, Sir, Funeral. I have heard of his accident Something abrupt in his Exit to be sure, a little Anglicism or so — But then I made no doubt, but the Family would take care to have it brought in Lunacy.
Tabby.
Lunacy, Sir! who told you then there was a Death in the family?

Wingrave

Oh, Sir; I never fail to enquire after their Health my Scouts are always on the Watch, I heard of it immediately. I have every thing constantly in readiness for any part of England, and nobody has better Scarves, gloves, and hatbands, handsome Coaches, and hearses, or more able Horses.

Tabby.

Horses! why the Church is almost next door, you know.

(8) Servant

Wingrave.

No matter for that, Sir; the less Occasion there is for them, so much the Grander to have them; It was but last week I buried Mr. Rennet the great Cheesemonger in Thames Street, and the Hearse and Six Stopt at the Church porch, before the Coach for the last Set of Mourners had drawn up to the Street door.

Tabby.

Rennet! why I don't believe he was ever in a Carriage in his whole Life time.

Wingrave

The Executors were resolv'd to have every thing handsome, and took down the Sign to make Room for the Hatchment — a Hearse and Six; and three Coaches and four I assure you; when folks are travelling to their long home: they can't have too good an Equipage, Sir; and none cleaner, neater, or genteeler than mine, in any part of England, Sir. — I am sure Mr Tobine would wish to have me put him into the Ground, Sir.

Taby.

No doubt on't.

Wing.

I did a great deal of Business for him in his Life time

Tabby.

Ay! What business did my partner employ you in, Mr Wingrave

Mr Wing.

I furnish'd three Houses at his Expence for Ladies in the new Buildings — One indeed had been furnish'd by the Lady's own Order — But then I sent in the Goods, and an Execution upon them together, and M.r Tobine afterwards paid the Charges of both.

    Tabby.

The Devil he did?

    Wingrave.

Yes, indeed, Sir. and it is a very common Practice among People of Quality. Several of the politest Houses are furnish'd in the same manner. Persons of Fashion in this Country always take great Care of the Benefit of their Tradesmen.

    Tabby.

So it seems my Friend; and then they give you an Opportunity of serving them in due Order in all your several Capacities — Let me see — what says your Hand Bill. <u>Upholsterer. Appraiser. Auctioneer and Undertaker.</u> — Ay, first of all, you supply them with Furniture, as an Upholsterer, then Value it as an Appraiser, or, knock it down as an Auctioneer, and soon after

       9
      Tobine
      D.r Truby
      M.rs Grog
      Nancy.

put them into the ground as you call it, as an Undertaker.

Wing.
Just so, Sir — and it was I that —

Enter Servant OP
Serv.ᵗ (to Tabby)
D.ʳ Truby desires to see you, in M.ʳ Tobines Room Sir.

Tabby.
I'll come to him.   (Exit Servant OP)
Well, M.ʳ Wingrave, I don't know that we shall want you at present.

Wingrave.
Presently at least I dare say, Sir. The Doctor and Apothecary has been here some time I find and we shall soon be wanted, I warrant you

Tabby.
Well, in that Case, we shall send for you

Wingrave.
Ten thousand thanks, Sir — I have had the pleasure of burying the Family for many Years

past, and I hope, I shan't lose your Custom. I never heard of any Complaints (10)

Tabby.

{Tabby. P.S. a paper}

No, I dare say.

Wingrave.

It was I that buried your good Lady, M.rs Tabby Sir — A prodigious fine Corpse, it wou'd have done you good to have seen her, Sir — M.rs Van, what d'ye call 'em, that her Husband keeps Pickled, and preserv'd in a Glass Case, does not look handsomer. a very genteel Funeral! — The Vault rather too low, and narrow, for your Family to be sure, but we made shift — placed M.rs Tabby in the Middle, her Grand=mother on the left hand, reserv'd room for your Honour on the right, and stowed the four little Children Edgeways o' top.

Tabby.

Mighty well manag'd — but I'm wanted M.r Wingrave Your Servant. <u>Exit OP.</u>

Wingrave

Your Servant Sir — I'le take care to have every thing

ready, your very humble Servant, Sir. P.S.

(R A)   Exeunt Severally.

Strip'd Chamber. Couch on

Tobine on a Couch in a night Gown.
Dr Truby, Mrs Grogram, Nancy & Servants.

Mrs Grog.
Do you think there are any hopes then Doctor

Dr Truby. (feeling his Pulse)
I don't like his Pulse, I assure you, put out your
Tongue if you please — Ah! very bad, very bad
truly.

Tobine.
I feel Extreamly weak and faint — all will soon
be over.

Mrs Grog.
Let me give him something heartning Doctor,
Some Godfreys Cordial, or pepper mint Water.

Nancy.
Take Comfort, Sir.

Tobine

Ah! my dear Nancy, how kind is it in you to Endeavour to administer it: Is it possible you can retain the least concern, or regard for so lost, so wretched a Creature!

Nancy

Heaven knows how much I feel for you; why did you not confide in your truest Friends, my whole Fortune would have been, and still is entirely in your disposal.

Tobine.

You are too generous to One so unworthy. How could I be blind to so much Excellence! I see my folly now it is too late, the thought of it is an additional Pang, and I regret the loss of Life, which I might have employ'd in redeeming my Character in your good Opinion. — Nay do not weep for me, I have not deserv'd it.

Enter Tabby P.S.

Tobine.

Well, Mr Tabby, what news of my friend Rattle.

Tabby.
The worst in the World
Tobine
Am I reserv'd for more misery before I depart then? Let it come at once. Make me acquainted with it, where is my friend?
Tabby.
Apprehended on Suspicion of wilfully giving you poison
Tobine.
Apprehended!
Tabby.
Yes, and if you should do otherwise than well, it is thought it will go very hard with him.
Tobine.
Heaven forbid! He is the best, the worthiest of Men. I alone am to blame, and pray be witness that I acquit him entirely
Tabby.
Ah! but his Confession before the Justices, I am afraid will make your Testimony of no Service

to him. In this Paper is an account of the ingredients of the mixture you have taken, and which he says he procur'd for you, the Doctor perhaps may be able to give an Opinion of them.

<u>D:ʳ Truby.</u>

Let me see (taking the paper) Arsenick, Hemlock Opium. — Zounds, here was enough to destroy twenty Men! — It is Surprizing he is alive at this moment. The Wine, and Brandy I suppose in some measure prevented the Operation of this Infernal Mixture; or, it must have dispatch'd him, almost immediately. Don't you feel very ill at present, Sir.

<u>Tobine.</u>

My bodily pain is trifling, but the agony of my mind is inexpressible.

<u>Nancy.</u> (a<u>part</u>.)

I cannot bear to see him so miserable

<u>D:ʳ Truby.</u>

Be quiet Simpleton (apa<u>rt</u>)

<u>Tobine.</u>

I charge you to take notice of my declaration

of my friends innocence, It was my own Act Entirely.

Tabby.

I am afraid he will be consider'd as an Accessary and yet, I believe what the Law can do to him is of very little Consequence; for the poor Lad is so affected with what he has done; and so distress't at hearing what you have suffer'd, that I don't think he will live to take his Trial.

Tobine.

Blest with two tender and Valuable friends, and to involve them both — the most faithful of Men, and the most affectionate of Women, in my ruin. — How dreadful is my Situation, Wantonly prodigal of my Life, and yet feeling myself a Wretch, and a Villain, the moment I am to part with it

Nancy.

Nay, I must, I will speak Comfort to him: I can withold no longer — Your own Life, Sir, the Life of your friend are neither of them in Danger.

How! what say you.
Dr Truby.
Ah! there is no stopping her.
Nancy.
Even my blushes shall not stop me from declaring to you, Sir; that the tender friend you see before you, and the person whom you cherish'd as the most faithful of Men are one and the same person.
Tobine.
Ha!
Nancy.
Who liv'd with you as a Companion in order to prevent the mischief you meditated against yourself, and who now rejoices in having accomplish'd her purpose.
Tobine.
Thou most generous of Women! thou dearest of Friends, is it possible.
Nancy.

Nancy.

Most certain!

Tobine.

And have not I taken poison then?

Dr Truby.

Not you indeed, Sir. — What you have taken was one of my Recipe's; If it has rummag'd you a little so much the better. A little Tartar Emitic for the Stomach. Some Jalap for the bowels and a few grains Extraordinary of Opium, are the whole Composition — And if you think it likely to be of Service to you, I hope you will recommend it to some of your mad friends, and acquaintance

Tabby.

Get a Patent for Vending it Doctor, and distribute it as largely as possible — for no Englishman have a right to throw away their Lives, when their Country has so much occasion for them.

Tobine.

The pains you have all taken to preserve mine deserves my warmest Thanks — but how shall I pay my gratitude here. (to Nancy)

When you are recover'd from your present Weakness, She'll tell you how — In the mean time resolve to make her as good a Husband, as she is likely to prove a good Wife, for she is fool enough to love you with all your absurdities. One promise however I must exact from each of you.

Nancy.

You have a right to Command us in every thing.

Tobine.

Do but name it, and be assur'd of our Compliance Sir.

Dr Truby.

Briefly this then — That you Madam, will never more quit the Petticoat, nor you Mr Tobine ever Die again, as long as you live.

The End.

Epilogue

The Critic's say and constantly repeat,
That Woman acting Man's a silly Cheat;
That ev'n upon the Stage it should not pass;
To which I say, a Critick is an Ass.
As Man, true Man, we could not well deceive
But we like Modish Things may make believe
Would it be thought I gave myself great Airs
To put my Manhood on a Foot with theirs?
Speak you that are Men, is my pride too great
To think you'd rather have with me a Tête,a tête.
   In this our Play what dangers have I run
What hair breadth Scapes, and yet the Prize have won
Is it a Prize, he may prove cross or Jealous
In <u>Marriage Lotteries</u> the knowing tell us.
Among our Modern Youths much danger lies
There are a hundred Blanks for one poor prize
Was I not bold ye Fair to undertake
To tame that wildest Animal a Rake?
To lead a Tyger in a Silken String
Hush the loud Storm, and clip the Whirlwinds Wing
My pride was piqu'd, all dangers I wou'd thro'
To have her way What will not Woman do.

The Papers swarm each day with Patent Puffers
For Smoaky Chimneys — Powders, Mouse traps, Snuffers
And I could Fame, as well as Fortune raise
To cure by Patent <u>La folie Angloise</u>
I'm sure you all my Nostrum will approve
By natures Guidance let your passions move
Drive out that Demon Gaming, by the Angel, Love.
But Ladies, if you wish to know my plan
By Stratagem, not force, attack your Man
By open War the Danger is increas'd
Use gentle means to sooth the Savage Beast.
If when his Blood boils o'er — Yours bubble too
Then all is lost, and there's the Devil to do
Puff! Puff! — Blown up at once the Lovers part
He Snaps his Chain, and Madam breaks her heart.
Hymen puts out his Torch, and Cupid blunts his Dart.
Thus ends the Farce, or Tragedy of Love
But Ladies, if your Sparks, are given to rove
From my Experience take one general Rule
Cool as he warms, and Love will never cool
If smoke prevails, and the choak'd flame is dying
Then gently fan it with some little Sighing

Then drop into the Flame a Tear or two.
And blazing up like Oil, twill burn him thro'
Then add kind looks, soft words, Sweet Smiles — no pout
And take my word the flame will ne'er go out
These with good humour mix'd, the balm of Life
Will be the best receipt for Maid or Wife

The End.

www.ingramcontent.com/pod-product-compliance
Lightning Source LLC
Chambersburg PA
CBHW031346160426
43196CB00007B/751